The of the Word

THE STORY OF DORCAS CAMACHO BYRD

ELIZABETH RIVERA

"Let us draw near to God with a sincere heart in full assurance of faith, having our hearts sprinkled to cleanse us from a guilty conscience and having our bodies washed with pure water. Let us hold unswervingly to the hope we profess, for he who promised is faithful. And let us consider how we may spur one another on toward love and good deeds" (Heb. 10:22–24 NIV).

Woman's Missionary Union
Birmingham, Alabama

Woman's Missionary Union
P. O. Box 830010
Birmingham, AL 35283-0010

Dewey Decimal Classification: 922.6
Subject Headings: BYRD, DORCAS CAMACHO
                  BYRD, EMERSON
                  BAPTISTS—BIOGRAPHY

Cover design by Janell E. Young
Cover illustration and inside illustrations by
Jane Chu Thompson

ISBN: 1-56309-235-2
W986104•0498•3M1

CONTENTS

1

POWER TO BELIEVE

"But godliness with contentment is great gain. For we brought nothing into the world, and we can take nothing out of it" (1 Tim. 6:6–7).

The baby was on the way and Mercedes had to get her sister Carmen to the hospital—quickly. The heat, bumpy roads, and horrible traffic made a simple task quite difficult. When they finally made it to the hospital—on time—Mercedes praised God. She felt just getting there had been a miracle.

The sun bathed Carmen Camacho and her son, Eliú [EL-E-OO] Jr., as the cool Caribbean breeze gently blew across them. Carmen was home again and the support of her family was comforting. She breathed deeply and smelled salt in the air. The luscious vegetation of Puerto Rico was soothing to Carmen's eyes. The Isla del Encanto (Enchanted Island) was just as beautiful as she remembered. God's creation was at the forefront wherever her eyes paused or rested.

Eliú Camacho, Carmen's husband, had received military orders to work with Special Forces in Panama and was not allowed to take his family with him during training. Mercedes and Manolo, Carmen's sister and father, were glad to have Carmen and Eliú Jr. stay with them for a while. They were especially happy Carmen's new baby would be born in Puerto Rico.

Carmen had made many plans before arriving in Puerto Rico. She and her husband had picked out the name for the baby, Mercy Marie, in honor of the baby's Aunt Mercedes and her great-grandmother. They had also planned how Eliú would be notified when the baby was born so he could fly home as soon as possible.

Plans are good, but flexibility allows God to polish them. As Mercedes drove her sister to the hospital, twisting and turning through traffic, she felt an impression from God that the baby's name should be Dorcas. But she dismissed the thought at the moment. She had to get Carmen to the hospital on time.

When Mercedes saw the baby, God's words came back to her. She exclaimed, "Why, she is a Dorcas! She really does look like a Dorcas!"

Carmen was tired but she spoke kindly to her sister. "That's too bad, Meche. I have already filled out the papers with the name Eliú and I picked to honor you and Grandmother."

Mercedes said a quick prayer and ran out of Carmen's hospital room to find someone who could change the papers.

That night, as Carmen tried to contact her husband through the Red Cross, Eliú walked into the hospital room. Carmen dropped the telephone and asked, "Why are you here? How did you know?"

As tears streamed down his face, Eliú answered. "God revealed it to me. I was in the Panamanian jungle, getting soaked by a torrential rainfall, when I suddenly became very happy. I burst out singing 'How Great Thou Art.' At that moment I knew my daughter had been born. I went to the company commander and asked for permission to come to Puerto Rico. That is why I am here."

Hesitantly, Carmen told her husband about the baby's name change. She was surprised at Eliú's delight. He told her about his sister who had died at age 12. Now he had a way to honor his sister. Her name had been Dorcas too.

Six months later Carmen, Eliú Jr., and baby Dorcas joined Eliú in Panama. When they arrived, Dorcas had a fever of 104°F. She was admitted to the hospital for close observation. Dorcas's parents prayed: "Dear Lord: This girl belongs to You. Please save her." Five days later she was released from the hospital without a diagnosis. Eliú and Carmen never forgot their vow to God. They had committed Dorcas's life to God and, throughout her life, reminded her that she was His child.

As a 3-year-old in the Dominican Republic, Dorcas often woke and began her day before the rest of the family. One day a neighbor was visiting Dorcas's mother, and the conversation turned quickly to Dorcas. "Do you know Dorquitas gets up very early every morning?" the neighbor asked.

"No, I didn't," Dorcas's mother honestly replied. "How do you know?"

"Well, every morning Dorquitas sits on the back porch and sings beautiful songs. My husband and I listen to her. I think she is going to be a singer."

Carmen's heart skipped a beat. Dorquitas, as Dorcas was affectionately called, was already witnessing to the neighbors and did not even know it. At that very moment Carmen prayed silently and thanked God that Dorcas was witnessing about their faith at such an early age.

At age 5, Dorcas enjoyed playing with friends in Puerto Rico. One day she was playing outside across the street from her home. Her mother stood on the porch and called to Dorcas, telling her to come inside. Then, just as she had called out to her daughter, Carmen saw a car speeding around the bend. Loudly and quickly she yelled, "Not now, Dorcas. Do not cross the street now. There is a car coming." Dorcas did not hear her mother nor did she see the car.

The car hit Dorcas and hurled her into the air. Carmen knew that if her child was still alive, the impact of the fall would surely kill her. So, she prayed, "Lord, please do not let anything happen to her."

Within seconds, a neighbor who was outside in the yard heard the mother scream and saw the speeding car hit the child. He ran into the street and caught Dorcas before she hit the ground. God had intervened in Dorcas's life. He had a specific and special plan for her.

As time went by, Dorcas realized she was set apart and dedicated to God. She was on this earth to serve and glorify Him. Her parents guided her to be godly and to find contentment serving Him.

2

POWER TO BECOME

"Be imitators of God, therefore, as dearly loved children and live a life of love, just as Christ loved us and gave himself up for us as a fragrant offering and sacrifice to God" (Eph. 5:1–2).

Dorcas? What kind of name is that?!" children taunted at school.

"My name is Dorcas Camacho. If you want to find my name in the Bible, look it up: Acts chapter 9, verse 36," she replied as her parents had taught her.

Church was central to Dorcas's family. As soon as they arrived at a new military base, they would begin searching for a new church to attend. Sometimes, if they were unable to find a church they were comfortable with, they would start their own. No matter what church they attended, Dorcas participated in the Girls in Action® (GA) missions organization.

Dorcas also enjoyed her international neighbors and felt as if the military was one big family. It never occurred to her that people could be classified by color or national origin. In the military everyone was the same.

Each base had a community center, one of Dorcas's favorite places. She attended many activities and parties and grew roots in community events. God would use these roots later in Dorcas's life to build a ministry.

Dorcas was the middle child of her family, but was identified as the oldest daughter. Eliú Jr., her brother, was the oldest and Abby was the baby in the family. Dorcas and Abby spent countless hours playing church. Dorcas played teacher, preacher, music director, and usher while Abby was the congregation. If Abby talked or started to doze off, Dorcas whispered, "Abby, Abby, that's not good. Stay awake. Pay attention and don't move."

Dorcas's parents taught the children that good decisions are godly decisions. God knew what was best for each of them in the long run, even if they didn't understand why at the time. The children learned to ask themselves, *What would please God?*

Dorcas always went to Baptist Women (now Women on Mission®) meetings with her mother on Thursdays. She participated in the program, prayed out loud, and drank coffee right along with all the women.

On Saturday mornings Dorcas and her family often ate a big brunch of pancakes and bacon. Then, they had a devotional, followed by family feedback time. Each family member said something positive about every other member. Afterwards they voiced any complaints or irritations about each other. No personal attacks or name-calling were allowed. This family time was simply a time to share information. Dorcas regularly directed statements to Abby: "I don't like it when you use my clothes without asking" and "I don't appreciate you using my things and not putting them back."

Today, Saturdays are a fond memory of childhood for Dorcas. She still eats pancakes and bacon for Saturday brunch, and she plans to continue the tradition of family time with her children.

As a child, Dorcas spent many summers in Puerto Rico where she established close family ties with cousins, aunts, uncles, and grandparents. Abuelo Manolo, Dorcas's grandfather, was the head of the family. He and Dorcas's aunts, Mercedes and Lina, influenced Dorcas and her cousins by their rich examples of Christian faith.

Grandfather Manolo was a kind man. He always had a warm greeting for everyone, and children delighted in seeing him because they knew he had candy for them.

Dorcas's aunts were forever constant when making decisions, basing them all on God's Word. They were so constant, in fact, that Dorcas could predict what they would say about a given situation. This provided Dorcas with boundaries, a sense of belonging, and security.

Puerto Rico's lavish green mountains, tropical rain forest El Yunque [EIY-unque], and the many beaches were favorite places for Dorcas and her family. No matter where they chose to visit, it was close to home. You can drive around the entire island of Puerto Rico in just a few hours. The long, lazy summer days with family are Dorcas's most treasured childhood memories.

Country fairs were a special event each summer in Puerto Rico's local towns. Dorcas's grandfather made ceramic pots and macramé to sell at the fairs and he allowed all the children to help. Together, they made 36 dozen pots for each fair. Grandfather assigned each person a task according to his or her ability. Dorcas's aunts painted the pots and added final touches. Everyone went to the country fairs with Grandfather to help sell the pots and macramé.

At the fairs, everyone was glad to see Grandfather Manolo and his family. Each family member took part in displaying and selling the macramé and pots. The grandchildren took charge of the money and made change because Grandfather Manolo was blind.

Dorcas's aunts, Mercedes and Lina, started three churches in Puerto Rico. Each aunt taught Dorcas life skills and set an example of a Christlike life for her. To Dorcas, these two sisters were like Mary and Martha in the Bible.

Aunt Mercedes taught Dorcas organizational skills. She was always doing something for her family, church, friends, and others in her community. She used every moment to be in service to others in Jesus' name. She was the Martha of the two aunts. She taught Dorcas how to give her life completely to God.

Aunt Lina was the happy aunt. She was more like Mary. For her, there was always time to sit and listen, to enjoy good conversation and company. She was known for her joyful nature. One of her favorite expressions was, "Isn't the Lord good?" Aunt Lina was always smiling and singing. Whenever she spoke about a friend or relative, she spoke with affection and love. She read her Bible daily and quoted Scripture constantly. Dorcas often wondered, *How did she ever learn so much?*

Dorcas had another aunt, Aunt Percy, her father's sister. She was always active in her church's Christian education and missions education programs. She was a member of Woman's Missionary Union® (WMU®) and attended meetings and participated in many of the missions education projects and programs. After Aunt Percy received her bachelor's and master's degrees when she was in her 40s, she became a school principal. Dorcas learned much from her Aunt Percy. Her determination and leadership were examples for Dorcas. She never wavered in her faith or departed from God's Word or His will.

Dorcas's mother and her aunts were the main female influences in her life. She received an inheritance of faith, commitment, dedication, and service to God from these godly women. Their examples would be Dorcas's standard of how to become a beautiful, godly young woman. These women set the pace for Dorcas's life.

3

POWER TO CHOOSE

"For it is by grace you have been saved, through faith—and this not from yourselves, it is the gift of God" (Eph. 2:8).

Dorcas had never been a Goody Two-shoes. She was mischievous, always pushing the limits set before her. These character traits have remained with her and keep her humble even as an adult. But they also led her to realize that she was a sinner.

When Dorcas was 12 years old, a musical group came to her church, First Baptist Church, Cocoa Beach, Florida. As a result, Dorcas accepted Christ as her personal Savior. The pastor, Reverend Medina, guided Dorcas through classes preparing her for baptism, and her Sunday School teacher involved her in missions by encouraging her to volunteer time at a children's home.

When Dorcas's father retired from the military, the family moved to Orlando, Florida. The transition from military to civilian life was difficult for Dorcas, then a preteen. She felt civilians treated her differently from her peers. While her church life was great, she was bullied at school. In order to cope, she developed a defense mechanism that wasn't pleasing to God. Dorcas's mother was concerned about Dorcas's intimidating nature. "Dorcas, your look alone could kill," she said. Dorcas purposefully used this look to intimidate peers and teachers alike.

"Fat lips, fat lips," taunted the children in sixth grade. Dorcas was constantly provoked by incessant name-calling. Once a boy, larger than his classmates, made fun of her in front of the whole class. Dorcas couldn't control her anger. She picked up a desk and threw it at him but missed. The chalkboard shattered instead.

Another classmate, Tonya, was a large, tough girl, who cursed, smoked, dressed, and acted older than the rest of the students. One day she picked on Dorcas and cut in line in front of her. Again, Dorcas's anger overwhelmed her. She punched Tonya so hard that she fell out of line. "You just wait," retorted Tonya.

"I'm not waiting for anything," Dorcas shot back. From that time on, people thought twice before they messed with Dorcas.

Those instances led Dorcas to believe that respect came from fighting. When Dorcas entered the seventh grade, all the students knew she was a good fighter. She was the king of the mountain, and her "kingdom" was always being challenged.

Once a girl said mean and untrue things about Dorcas, trying to provoke a fight. The girl went to Dorcas's locker and said, "I'm going to beat you up. Right here, right now."

"No, not here, not now," responded Dorcas.

"Yeah, now."

"OK, you start it and I'll finish it."

The girl stepped forward, but Dorcas was ready. She punched the girl in the face over and over. Dorcas was used to fighting with boys, but this girl didn't fight like a boy. She pulled Dorcas's hair and scratched her face and arms. Dorcas was hurting, but she had learned from the boys never to cry. Her opponent, however, became hysterical when she realized she was bleeding. The girl's tears brought an end to the fight. Dorcas opened her locker, got her books, and went to class.

Before the end of class, both girls found themselves sitting in the principal's office, expecting to be suspended. When the girls spoke, Dorcas said, "I didn't start it.

She pushed me and fought me first." Just then, the girl walked over and hugged Dorcas. Then she apologized to Dorcas for starting the fight.

"I'm so sorry, Dorcas," the girl said.

"Well, I'm sorry too, for having to do that to you," Dorcas replied.

The surprised principal decided not to call Dorcas's parents and not to suspend the girls from school. The matter was never mentioned again.

Another time, when Dorcas was getting on the school bus, a girl shoved her, causing her to fall into another student. Dorcas turned around and punched the girl in the nose. The girl fell in a puddle of blood, and Eliú Jr., Dorcas's brother, grabbed his sister by the shirt, pulling her onto the bus. This was not the first time, or the last, that he intervened on her behalf.

This fight didn't end so quickly, though. The injured girl's brother told his buddies that he was going to beat up Dorcas. Eliú Jr. got word of the threat and sought out the boy. "I don't fight Dorcas's battles," Eliú Jr. said. "But if you touch her, I'll beat you up. The fight is between our sisters. Besides, you're too old to be fighting Dorcas."

Eliú Jr. had a way of getting Dorcas out of trouble. He kept his distance and allowed her the freedom to make her own choices, but he always showed up when Dorcas most needed him.

As a new Christian, Dorcas wanted to be a good example of a Christian young person. She didn't want to fight, but it was hard to overcome the temptation. She had strong opinions and would voice them, even at risk of being rejected by her peers. Fighting was a tried-and-true defense mechanism.

Dorcas knew fighting was not godly and she needed to find a better way to assert herself. *How could God possibly use her when she fought? Would her testimony ever be useful if she was serving in church on the weekend and fighting at school during the week? Did God understand the position she was in at school?* These questions bothered Dorcas, but she couldn't find an answer.

4

POWER TO SERVE

"Therefore, I urge you, brothers, in view of God's mercy, to offer your bodies as living sacrifices, holy and pleasing to God—which is your spiritual worship. Do not conform any longer to the pattern of this world, but be transformed by the renewing of your mind. Then you will be able to test and approve what God's will is—his good, pleasing and perfect will" (Rom. 12:1–2).

Christmas, when Dorcas was in the eighth grade, set a new course of life for the Camacho family. Her father felt called into the ministry, and he explained that the whole family needed to feel a desire to serve Christ in order for him to act on his calling.

Each family member prayed individually about it and felt affirmation. They all accepted Eliú Camacho's calling as their own. The children understood that Christians are servants, so they committed to do whatever they could to help build up the church, the body of Christ.

When God provided an opportunity, they interpreted it as an expression of His will. If any of them were asked to speak, sing, teach, or otherwise serve in the church, they believed it was part of God's plan. Dorcas's mother acknowledged her children's gifts and talents. She supported them by encouraging them to pray and serve others. When a need was mentioned, Carmen would often say, "Dorcas can do that." So, Dorcas approached tasks such as praying, cleaning, and tending to guests in a positive way. She often thought, *Wow, I really can do that!*

Later the family moved to Biloxi, Mississippi, where they started a Hispanic church and Dorcas's father commuted to New Orleans Baptist Theological Seminary. This way he was able to get the education he needed to prepare himself for full-time ministry while gaining practical experience.

Dorcas was glad to have a chance to start over at a new school in Biloxi. Nobody in her new school would know that she could defend herself by fighting. Her cousin Fito, who moved with the family to Biloxi, was a good influence on Dorcas. He was friendly and athletic, and together he and Dorcas established good reputations. Dorcas joined the choir, and in ninth grade she won the talent show. She was part of the pep squad for basketball, and had only a distant memory of her fighting past.

Dorcas gladly took on any responsibility handed her at church. She sang, led Bible studies, enjoyed church fellowships, and was always available to help. Her first solo was at First Baptist Church, Biloxi, when she sang "Go, Tell It on the Mountain." Eventually she became the director of music at the Hispanic mission.

Dorcas always got nervous before a solo. Her mother comforted her, but she would also say, "God will take that talent away from you, unless you use it when He says to—when it is needed." Dorcas noticed that God only used her singing when she prayed and asked Him to use her as His vessel to touch someone through the words of the song.

As she continued to mature, Dorcas began to understand the values her parents had emphasized since she was a child. She began to identify and practice the main principles that she would base her life on—humility, joy, and thankfulness.

But Dorcas still had difficulty controlling her anger. Her mother kept reminding Dorcas that a Christian cannot be two different persons. A Christian is a Christian at all times, regardless of place or circumstance. When Dorcas used her intimidating glare, her mother would say, "That's not the kind of look or attitude a Christian should have. You must learn to deal with conflict and anger in a different way."

Dorcas didn't know how to stop. Intimidation was a quick and easy way to gain respect. She wasn't fighting anymore. Wasn't that enough?

When Dorcas was in the tenth grade, the family moved to New Orleans, Louisiana, where her father served as pastor of Primera Iglesia Bautista Hispanoamericana. Moving to a new church was not difficult for Dorcas. She could count on filling her calendar with Christian events: youth camps and rallies, lock-ins, roller-skating parties, and many other church and associational youth activities. And, there would be boys there. But school changes were not always smooth for Dorcas.

Her father reminded the family of their call to servanthood. "We have to do missions and serve," he would constantly say. Every morning the family prayed for the conversion of people in the mission. The Camachos looked for Hispanics everywhere and invited them to the mission.

On the first Sunday, 20 people attended. Dorcas felt a closeness to these people and a desire to minister to them. Many people made decisions to follow Christ and took their places of service alongside the Camacho family.

One man from the community was totally transformed. When Dorcas's family first visited in his home, they found him drinking beer and watching television. He was so absorbed in his activities that he ignored their visit with him. Later that very same night, however, he accepted Christ as his personal Savior while watching a religious television program that came on at 2:00 A.M. He had wanted to turn off the program, but found himself unable to. The next Sunday he came to the mission and made his public profession of faith. Less than three months after the man accepted Christ, he rented a storefront and started a coffeehouse, providing Christian movies and music for military people from Keesler Air Force Base in Biloxi.

Another man in the community was transformed literally right before Dorcas's eyes. His wife had suffered through several episodes of his abuse before meeting the Camacho family. Through association with them and other members of the mission, the man became a Christian.

The complete transformation Christ made in the lives of these men was a great witness to Dorcas. Watching them helped her mature as a Christian.

The process of growing up and maturing in faith was a normal one for Dorcas. As a preteen, she was definitely not a girl people would label as a future missionary. In fact, most adults would have never dreamed it possible. She was mischievous and always seemed to have a plan to get her way. Dorcas's parents, however, loved her and knew that God had a plan for her life. They made sure that she knew it too.

She hadn't gone to school in New Orleans long before a crisis occurred during a home economics class. The teacher told the students to pick a sewing machine and sit down in front of it. When Dorcas picked one and sat down, a girl came and told Dorcas to move out of the way. Dorcas calmly repeated the teacher's instruction, but the girl picked Dorcas up and started beating her.

While this girl hit Dorcas, something strange happened. Dorcas suddenly realized she didn't remember how to fight. Her fingers didn't automatically curl into powerful fists as before. She couldn't remember how to make that intimidating glare she had used so well just a year ago. As the girl struck her again, Dorcas cried out for joy. "It's gone. It's gone." The other girls stared at Dorcas, then began laughing. They had no idea why she was so happy.

As the girls sat in the principal's office, Dorcas approached the girl. She said, "I'm thankful I didn't fight back. I know you're tougher than me, and I'm glad I didn't fight back." The girl laughed at her and thought she was crazy.

That day Dorcas knew that God had helped her overcome her desire to fight and intimidate others. She had learned to depend on God to work out problems in her life.

5

POWER TO CHANGE

"Trust in the Lord with all your heart and lean not on your own understanding; in all your ways acknowledge him, and he will make your paths straight" (Prov. 3:5–6).

Dorcas was 15 years old and full of mischief when the family moved to New Orleans. While she didn't look for criminal activities, she did delight in carefree antics that nearly drove the adults around her insane. Learning to drive was no exception to Dorcas's mischief.

One day Dorcas's father told her that she could drive the van to church and then give the keys to the minister of youth. Dorcas was determined to prove that she could drive well enough not only to have fun but also to be of service. So, when she got to the church, she kept the keys and told Marta, the minister of youth, "I'll pick up the youth and bring them to church. Come ride with me."

Marta's stomach began to ache as she rode in the van with Dorcas. The ride lasted only about 20 minutes, but it seemed to last an eternity. Dorcas made U-turns, drove up on curbs, and darted out in front of other drivers that she did not even notice were on the road.

Finally, Marta could stand it no longer. She ordered, "Dorcas, pull over and give me the keys. I'll talk to your father when we get back."

Dorcas gladly gave the keys to Marta. She had actually frightened herself. The hard part came later, after Marta talked to Dorcas's father.

"Dorcas, give me your license," he demanded. "I'll be keeping it for you for a while." Dorcas did not dare comment or ask when she would get her license back. For three interminable months, she relied on others to drive her wherever she needed to go.

Hardheaded determination kept Dorcas from learning much from that experience, though. She soon forgot how afraid she had made herself. When she had her license again, she thought about how easily the adults had overreacted.

Not long after that, Dorcas and Abby asked for permission to go to a wedding where they could see a boy Dorcas wanted to meet. Early in the week, they began to plan what they would wear, say, and do.

When Saturday finally came, the girls spent all day getting ready. They both looked beautiful by early evening as they sat waiting for their father to come home and take them to the wedding. However, when the telephone rang, they knew he was calling to say he would be home late.

Dorcas and Abby waited patiently, hoping their dad would hurry home. They had to get to the wedding early enough to meet the boy before some other girl did! An hour or more went by and their father called again. Unexpected complications had further delayed him.

The sisters began whining, crying, and begging their mother to let them go alone. After all, Dorcas could drive them there. No one remembered that the only car available had a stick shift. Dorcas knew nothing about shifting gears and using a clutch. Relentless badgering finally wore their mother down and she agreed to let them go.

Jerking, stopping, starting, jerking—Dorcas and Abby made it to the wedding on the other side of New Orleans. While talking to a group of friends, Dorcas gathered attention by bragging about driving the stick-shift car to the wedding. Before she knew it, she was taking friends for a ride to show off her supposed newfound skill.

But then, the car stalled out on the railroad track. Dorcas got so nervous she couldn't get the car started. She and her friends were stuck! Finally, all the girls got out of the car, and in their beautiful dresses pushed the car off the track. Embarrassed, scared, and with adrenaline pumping, Dorcas was finally able to get the car started again.

By the time the girls got back to church, everyone had left, which meant Dorcas would have to drive her friends home, far across town. Dorcas and Abby arrived home at 11:30 P.M., the latest they had ever stayed out. Their mother sat in a chair crying so hard that she barely noticed them arrive. She was scared that her daughters had been in an accident and had no one to help them. When Dorcas and Abby kissed and hugged her, she would not let them go, and thanked God they were alive and well. She did not know how close they came to being run over by a train.

Dorcas's tendency toward mischief extended to all areas of her life. She thought Hispanic youth camps were always the best fun. One year she and her friend Luisa, the camp director's daughter, stayed up all night on Monday night. About 4:00 A.M. they had run out of things to talk about, so they took showers, dressed, and put on makeup. But that only took an hour. They were ready a full hour before everyone else would be up.

Dorcas and Luisa decided to wake the others. They went to the gym where the sound system was and turned it on full blast. Using tambourines to increase the level of noise even more, they sang, "Rise and shine, and give God the glory." They sang for an hour at the top of their lungs, waking everybody in the camp and winning angry stares and comments for the day.

That afternoon Dorcas and Luisa had trouble staying awake, so they decided, along with two boys, to skip the afternoon activities. The four teenagers were intelligent people, but it never occurred to any of them that they would be missed!

They went for a walk in the woods to stay awake. As they came to an open area, they saw a car far in the distance. The camp leaders were out looking for them! Dorcas, Luisa, George, and Tony all tried to hide behind a skinny tree. The leaders, of course, saw them and took them back to camp. The rest of the afternoon they had to stay in their rooms with no air-conditioning while everyone else went swimming.

Camp that summer was full of many other mischievous antics and opportunities to push the limits of the rules. Dorcas took advantage of every one. But she also took advantage of the opportunity to grow in her relationship with Christ.

Friday, the last day of camp, was always a special day. All the girls decked out in their best outfits and wore perfume for the talent show, which was the major social event of the week. This Friday night turned out to be one of the best nights of Dorcas's life. She, Eliú Jr., and her cousin Fito rededicated their lives to God. Dorcas made a conscious decision to serve Him above all else with all of her mind, body, and soul.

Dorcas never heard an audible voice, noticed a particular moment, felt a knock on her head, or encountered any other extraordinary event. Instead, she experienced a gradual, constant, step-by-step, day-by-day, closer walk with God.

While Dorcas's teenage years were full of mischief, they were not as troublesome as her preteen years. Because she had totally committed her life to God, she never followed the crowd and could not understand those who did. But some questions still troubled her: *Why do Christian girls, teens, and women go along with styles that are not modest and godly? Why do they use language that puts themselves and others down?*

Whenever she found herself in situations beyond her own understanding, Dorcas acknowledged God and trusted Him to make her paths straight. She learned that God can and does accomplish extraordinary things through ordinary people who commit themselves to Him.

6

POWER TO EXPLORE

"But seek first his kingdom and his righteousness, and all these things will be given to you as well" (Matt. 6:33).

The campus of Samford University in Birmingham, Alabama, was beautiful. Its stately buildings, rolling hills, and luscious landscaping transported Dorcas to a fantasyland where all her dreams could come true. She wanted to use her musical talent for God and in His service. She was convinced that the only way for this to happen was to earn a bachelor's degree in music.

Although she had been ministering with her voice since she was 14, Dorcas believed she could not offer true service to God if her college education was not in the same field. But college life turned out to be much less than a fairy tale for Dorcas. Her classes at Samford were difficult. She literally had nightmares about college algebra. She couldn't understand anything. She was unable to relate her studies to her experience. She felt stuck in mud with her wheels spinning at full speed.

Cultural experiences also tried her faith but also gave her opportunities to grow to be more Christlike. One such time was when Alexis, her cousin, was her roommate. Alexis was born and raised in Puerto Rico and preferred speaking Spanish, her native language, over English much of the time.

One night the girls found a note on their dorm room door. The note said: *We do not want you to speak Spanish, nor do we want to hear Spanish music coming from your room or anywhere else on campus.* It was signed, *The Third Floor.*

"They hate us. They hate us," Alexis said, as she began sobbing uncontrollably. Dorcas did not know which was worse, the note or Alexis's devastation. Dorcas decided to take Alexis to a dear friend, Keith Boswell, who had grown up as a missionaries' kid (MK) in Peru. He was supportive and led Dorcas and Alexis to pray about the situation. When the girls returned to their room, they wrote on sticky notes the familiar Bible passage about love (1 Cor. 13). They signed the notes, *We love you, Dorcas and Alexis.* Then they stuck one note on every door of the third floor.

The next morning during breakfast at the cafeteria, many students who lived on the third floor of Dorcas's and Alexis's dorm came to the girls' table to hug them and tell them they loved them too! Dorcas and Alexis never found out who wrote the note to them; but they did learn that a loving, Christlike response is the best solution to cultural differences and misunderstandings.

At the beginning of her second year in college, Dorcas took some aptitude tests to determine her strengths and weaknesses. The counselor gave her a list of suggested careers based on the results. She chose social work because, from what she understood, social workers did what all Christians should do—serve others. Samford didn't have a social work program, so Dorcas moved home to live with her parents in Pompano Beach, Florida, where she could attend a community college.

Everything began to click. Dorcas began to understand better what she was doing and where her college education was leading her. She did so well in her classes that she was able to take a job to help pay for her tuition and living expenses. She cleaned houses in her spare time and learned another valuable lesson—a modest home would be more than enough for her. Big houses, she decided, are just too difficult to maintain!

Since Dorcas was living with her parents, she continued to benefit from their example of Christlike living. These were not always the easiest and most comfortable lessons to learn.

One day Dorcas's cousins were visiting with the family. Dorcas, Abby, and their cousins spent all day in the sun. That evening, they were sunburned and hungry. Dorcas's mother made a wonderful spaghetti dinner with bread, salad, and all the trimmings. Just as everyone had finished eating, the phone rang.

"Brother Eliú," a woman's voice greeted Dorcas's father. "I was wondering what time you are coming over for dinner. I have spent all day cooking my traditional German dishes for you and your family."

Dorcas's mother and the girls listened to Eliú's response. "We were just about to leave," he replied. "We will be there at 7:00 P.M. to enjoy that wonderful meal you have so graciously prepared for us."

Dorcas's parents had forgotten about agreeing to eat with their neighbor, but they did not want to offend the dear Christian woman. Dorcas, Abby, and the cousins complained to no avail that they had already eaten quite well. Eliú responded, "You have five minutes to be in the car and prepare yourselves to eat again."

When they entered the woman's home, they found a beautiful German feast and a house with no air-conditioning. The girls' sunburns intensified and their stomachs were still stuffed. Even though they felt like crying, they knew there was only one way out. Eat. Eat. Eat.

Dorcas's parents also taught her how to budget her money. Her father helped her figure out the amounts for her tithes first, then savings, and then debt payments, like her car. She was also expected to give a certain percentage of her earnings for household expenses. Her parents explained that even though they didn't need her money to cover her living expenses with them, she needed to learn to pay her own way. They knew she would move out on her own one day and would have to deal with rent payments, utilities, groceries, and other living expenses. They didn't want her to be caught off guard and not know how to manage money wisely.

The algebra nightmare pursued Dorcas all the way through college. She registered for the class four times and dropped it every time. Her last semester of college she went to her professor and explained that it was the last class she needed to graduate. He could only wish her luck.

The class was a requirement. She had done poorly all semester and both saw little hope for her passing with even the lowest grade.

Dorcas only knew of one other avenue—a miracle. She asked everyone she knew to pray. She went to church and asked the congregation to pray for her. When she took the exam, she was calm and felt God's presence. She passed the test with a C.

Dorcas went straight to church to tell her good news. Their prayers were answered. She would graduate!

This experience taught Dorcas the importance of never giving up. She learned that it does not matter how intelligent a person is or how many resources are available; God is always faithful. Through Dorcas's perseverance and dependence on God, she met her goals and accomplished her dream.

Dorcas graduated from Florida Atlantic University with a bachelor's degree in social work. After graduation Dorcas accepted a position working with battered women in the field of domestic violence. When her father told her that the Southern Baptist Theological Seminary in Louisville, Kentucky, offered a graduate degree program in social work, Dorcas applied. The family was moving to California, however, and Dorcas moved with them. She got her first full-time, full-fledged job as a bilingual outreach counselor with the Young Women's Christian Association (YWCA) assisting with migrant workers in Fresno, California.

The women Dorcas worked with lived in terrible conditions, and worse than that, their husbands often beat them. She told the women that they could die, but this had little effect. The thought even seemed to appeal to some of the women. However, the second alternative Dorcas told them about seemed to them a worse fate than death. They might live and lose their children to the state which would protect them from an abusive father.

At night Dorcas taught parenting classes based on what she had learned in school. She also counseled abusive men in support groups. Although she was not allowed to present the gospel, she could tell them about her life and relationship with Christ if they asked.

When the women questioned Dorcas's personal experience with domestic violence, she explained that because her family members were Christians, they loved and respected each other. Her father respected her mother, just as she respected him. The women were always surprised at the response, so their next question was, "Then why do you want to help me?" This question enabled Dorcas to seize the opportunity to tell the women about the love of Christ in her.

Once a violent husband, whose wife had a restraining order against him, came home while Dorcas was counseling with the wife. He pushed the door open with such force that both Dorcas and the wife shuddered with fear. But Dorcas felt the peace of God's Holy Spirit lift her from her seat. She almost pounced on the man, offering a strong, friendly handshake and a big smile. "It's a pleasure to meet you," Dorcas said. "I bet you could tell me a lot about the work you do. It seems very difficult," she heard herself say.

After a while the man calmed down enough that Dorcas risked mentioning some of the other difficulties he was experiencing and offered her counseling services to him. Much to her surprise, he showed up at the counseling center. Eventually, the couple got back together and their children were returned from foster care.

7

POWER TO GROW

"And whatever you do, whether in word or deed, do it all in the name of the Lord Jesus, giving thanks to God the Father through him" (Col. 3:17).

When Dorcas enrolled at the Southern Baptist Theological Seminary in Louisville, Kentucky, in August 1989, her immediate need was to find a job. As she walked on campus, she saw a YWCA sign advertising help wanted in the area of domestic violence. Dorcas ran all the way from the Carver Social Work building to her dorm room to call about the job.

Part of her was in utter disbelief. She thought she could hear Aunt Lina's voice say, *Isn't the Lord good?!* Even thousands of miles away, Dorcas felt the strength and support of her family. This job was tailor-made for her because of her job experience in California and her beginning graduate studies in social work. There was no question about her being suited for the job. She burst in the dorm and announced she had found a job. When her roommate started asking questions, Dorcas silenced her by saying, "I just have to call and tell them." Dorcas called the YWCA and explained her background and experience.

When she went for the job interview, she knew all the right answers. She spoke about the cycle of violence using key terms that she had learned in school. When she was called back for a second interview, Dorcas took some of the materials that she had used on her job in California. Everyone agreed; Dorcas was the right person for the job.

Her job involved working in hospital advocacy. She would have to wear a beeper and go to the hospital when they called her. She would interview victims and take photographs for documentation to be used later in legal procedures. She would be on call from Sunday at midnight through Friday.

The first few weeks on the job, Dorcas didn't get a single call. She became concerned about whether or not she had really been employed! When she called the personnel office of the YWCA, they assured her that she should not worry. Volunteers were helping at all times, but when they needed her—and that time would come at the most inconvenient moment—they would call her.

Sure enough, she got a hefty check for nothing but wearing a beeper those first few weeks. And as promised, she began receiving calls at the worst times imaginable. Often, she would be called out of a sound sleep to take photographs of women who had been horribly beaten, almost beyond recognition.

Sometimes the sight of blood mixed with the smell of alcohol was too much for Dorcas. She could only hold her breath long enough to say hello and leave. She would beg nurses to help her take the photographs, then wait for the victim to be cleaned up a bit to get her story.

During times off, Dorcas would lay out at the pool and tease passersby, "Nice job I've got, huh?" Once again God had provided for Dorcas. She kept the job all three years she attended seminary.

While visiting her parents during Christmas in 1991, Dorcas's last year at seminary, her father suggested that she place her résumé on file with the seminary's placement office and send out résumés to various Southern Baptist agencies. She followed his advice and had her first interview during spring break, just before graduation, with Chicago's Metropolitan Baptist Association.

The position was for a home missionary

church and community minister to work with Cook County Hospital, which served a community of little resources and revenue. In many cases, there was a single shower for an entire ward of hospital patients, and no soap. Her job would involve connecting volunteers from churches in the association with the hospital to help meet needs such as obtaining food vouchers for special diets, arranging special events, and preparing gift bags with essential hygiene items for the different wards.

After a second interview, Dorcas was offered and accepted the job. She was scheduled to start in August 1992. Upon graduation, Dorcas started the Home Mission Board (now the North American Mission Board) process for being commissioned, a job requirement.

Dorcas's job brought tough challenges as well as tender experiences. Once when a church group passed out hygiene kits, a patient began to cry. Some members of the group thought they had offended her. The patient later confided to Dorcas that she had been praying for two weeks that someone would come and minister to her. She was a Christian and had been deeply touched by the simple gift of a bar of soap. When other people heard that story, they became involved in additional ministries to help the hospital patients. Several weeks later that same church group sent

Dorcas a huge box of soap for the hospital.

In June 1993, Dorcas flew to Houston for her commissioning service as a home missionary. Once there, she learned that she would be giving a 5-minute testimony during the service. She spoke about her family, her understanding of servant-hood, and her hope that her work would lead others in the church to become involved in ministry.

Jim Herrington, the associational direc-tor of missions for Union Baptist Associa-tion, was in that service. A few months later, he called Dorcas and told her about the Baptist Mission Centers in Houston's inner city that home missionary Mildred McWhorter had started. Jim had been looking for someone to fill the director's position for the centers since Mildred's retirement. He was convinced Dorcas was the person for the job.

Dorcas wasn't interested. She had just started her work in Chicago and liked her job. She didn't even want to consider a change at this time.

Jim asked her to pray about it for two weeks before she gave him an answer. As she did, she felt the Holy Spirit reprimand her. She had been caught not even con-sidering God's will. Surely she could think and pray about it. After all, she knew

God's way is always best. It's a guaranteed pattern to success.

Dorcas called her parents and Emerson Byrd, a man she had met while at seminary. She asked them to pray with her about the need in Houston. Phone calls came and went and still Dorcas did not feel led to consider going to Houston. In October, Jim Herrington called and asked her to visit the centers before making a final decision. Dorcas agreed and made plans to go to Houston to see the Baptist Mission Centers.

While she was there, she and Jim went to Joy Mission Center. Volunteers were everywhere, preparing food bags, giving out clothes, working with children. There were more than 200 people in the worship service. Dorcas was impressed and moved by the needs of the community and the dedication of the volunteers.

The other centers were closed that day, but they drove by and saw the properties. When they arrived back at the association, Dorcas was surprised to be greeted by a group of men and women. She had no idea they would be interviewing her; and, in fact, didn't realize she was actually being interviewed for the job. Had she realized that this was an official interview, she would have been nervous. Dorcas was happy in Chicago and still had no desire to come to Houston, although she was in awe of the work of the Baptist Mission Centers.

When one of the committee members asked her why she wanted to come to Houston, Dorcas answered, "I don't want to come to Houston. Why do you want to bring me here?" This opened up a conversation about their vision and hope for the centers. By the end of this interview, Dorcas was beginning to feel God speaking to her about coming to Houston.

Dorcas could see a great opportunity to help average church members become Christlike servants and express how God had transformed their lives. More than anything, Dorcas wanted to help Christians understand that they are called to serve. The Baptist Mission Centers were a perfect place to involve different people with all kinds of gifts and abilities in service to God.

Dorcas went back to the hotel and called her friend Emerson and told him about the people and their work, and she told him she was feeling God's leadership to move to Houston. Emerson assured her of his support in whatever she felt God leading her to do.

After returning to Chicago, Dorcas called Union Baptist Association and accepted the job offer. She was invited to a formal interview to continue the hiring process. She began her new job on April 1, 1994.

8

POWER TO BE HONEST

"Love . . . always protects, always trusts, always hopes, always perseveres" (1 Cor. 13:6,7).

Should I go to Southwestern Seminary in Fort Worth, Texas, or to Southern Seminary in Louisville, Kentucky, for a master's degree in social work? Emerson Byrd asked himself. He had just come back from The Gambia, a country in Africa, where he had served two years as a missionary journeyman. Emerson decided to visit a friend, Larry Daniels, who was attending Southern Seminary. *It would be a good idea to see the school and get a feel for it,* Emerson thought.

Larry took Emerson to one of his classes and promptly introduced him to Dorcas, a classmate. Her eyes lit up when Emerson mentioned he was an MK from Guatemala. Luisa Reyes, one of Dorcas's best friends, was Guatemalan, as were her first high school sweetheart and many church friends from New Orleans. She had many fond memories of the kindness of Guatemalan Christians. Dorcas and Emerson talked about Guatemala until the class started.

Emerson had become a Christian at the age of 9 while attending a Royal Ambassadors camp in Guatemala. He went to American private schools in Guatemala, but he spoke Spanish at church and in the community and watched Spanish television. Though he was an American, Emerson was totally immersed in Guatemalan culture. He enjoyed corn tortillas; black beans; and tostadas layered with meat, slaw, and colorful beets. While on furlough one year, young Emerson wondered if Guatemalans would understand television programs if his family took a television from the US back to Guatemala. He did not consider that the programs are transmitted in Spanish, having nothing to do with the television set!

As he grew, Emerson felt he was somewhat different from others, someone with a special culture that afforded him higher aspirations and opportunities. As a preteen, Emerson looked forward to the day he would be able to enjoy all the youth group activities at church. He thought, *They have so much fun!* But when the time finally came, Emerson passed up youth activities so he could help start a new church. During his last three years in Guatemala, he worked at the new congregation.

After college, Emerson sought experiences outside the Hispanic and Anglo cultures. He was still in the process of settling his identity. That had led him to The Gambia. As a college student, he had felt being an MK and being fluent in Spanish limited rather than enhanced his talents and experience. Later he came to realize that his Guatemalan upbringing and knowledge of Spanish were wonderful tools God could use. His experiences and abilities would enable him to make a larger contribution to missions and ministry.

Dorcas and Emerson met during her last year in seminary and his first. When Emerson started seminary in January, he visited several churches in search of a home church. One Sunday he visited St. Matthews Baptist Church Hispanic Mission. During Sunday School, he met Dorcas's sister, Abby, and Brenda, a Guatemalan friend of Dorcas's. Dorcas was at a local Lutheran church where she worked in the nursery. When she arrived at St. Matthews for the worship service, Abby and Brenda met her at the front door, raving about a visitor who was cute and spoke Spanish perfectly! When they mentioned he was a new seminary student and an MK from Guatemala, Dorcas replied calmly, "Oh, yes, I've met him."

Just getting over someone else at the time, Dorcas didn't have romantic thoughts about the handsome newcomer, Emerson Byrd. But when she greeted him, she made a lasting impression. Emerson remembers that Dorcas was very attractive, slender, and petite. She wore a cream-colored dress that brought out her natural coloring. After church Dorcas invited Emerson for lunch and to play board games along with the usual crowd.

Emerson quickly became part of the group. They enjoyed spending their free time together going to movies and out to eat. Emerson joined the Hispanic mission because he felt most comfortable there among the group and language.

In August, Dorcas left for her job at Cook County Hospital in Chicago, Illinois. In September, her friends from seminary came to visit, and Emerson was part of the group. Everyone had a great time staying up all night playing games and talking.

Why don't we realize what we have until we lose it? Emerson thought. He hadn't realized how much he had in common with Dorcas and how much he enjoyed her friendship in particular until she moved away. They were both third-culture kids.

They had grown up in a culture different from that of their parents. They were both bilingual and had formed an identity based on both the Anglo and Hispanic cultures. They were both from families who had dedicated their lives to full-time Christian ministry. Both families had taught their children that to be a Christian was to be a minister to others—to serve and help others. They had both enjoyed relationships with other internationals. Both were active in their church and had chosen the same church while at seminary. They enjoyed mutual friends. Both had learned through each new experience the next step God wanted them to take. Emerson, like Dorcas, felt a stronger calling to serve God in ministry with each new experience.

We would complement each other so well. We would be an asset to each other in God's purpose for our lives, Emerson continued his thoughts. *But, is it too late?* Dorcas had moved to Chicago and had no idea of Emerson's love for her.

In January, Emerson and the rest of the group, including a new girl Dorcas hadn't met, went to Chicago for another visit. Meanwhile in Chicago, Dorcas had made many other new friends. She was excited for her seminary friends to meet her Chicago friends. Their night of fun was just

beginning at 1:00 A.M. Coffee, hot choco-
late, and soft drinks kept everyone awake
as they played the guitar and told jokes. At
5:00 A.M. they all drove to Lake Michigan
to see the sun rise. When they returned to
the apartment at 9:00 A.M., they dropped to
the floor and slept until noon. The whole
weekend was one big party.

Emerson realized, however, that Dorcas
had no clue about his feelings for her
when she asked him if he planned to start
dating the new girl in the group. She
thought he was interested in another girl!

By Monday Dorcas's seminary friends
were back at school, but her friend Patti
could not get something off her mind.
She wrote Dorcas a letter, telling her that
Emerson was in love with Dorcas. Emerson also wrote to Dorcas, not knowing
that Patti had already written her. His letter was vague, only asking to talk to her
about some changes in his life. Dorcas
didn't know what to expect, since the letters sounded quite different.

The next weekend, on the way back from
a youth camp in Tennessee, Dorcas stopped
in Louisville to visit her friend Brenda. Not
realizing that she was creating an uncomfortable situation, Brenda had invited both
Emerson and Patti to her home while Dorcas was there. Dorcas knew that Emerson

was not aware of the correspondence she and Patti had shared. And Emerson had already planned to visit Dorcas the following weekend in Chicago to declare his love for her. Dorcas and Emerson both acted nervous and awkward. They talked about the youth camp, but neither mentioned their impending meeting.

The next weekend was Valentine's Day. Emerson, his roommate, and his roommate's girlfriend, who was coming in from Canada, were visiting in Chicago. Emerson brought flowers for Dorcas, but she accepted them flippantly. She did not intend to make this conversation easy for Emerson! If he loved her, he would have to express his feelings clearly. Emerson was prepared to do exactly that. He asked for some time alone with her.

Sitting with Emerson on a bench next to a fountain at the apartment building, Dorcas listened carefully as he started by telling her how he admired her qualities, listing them one by one. He told her how much he loved her and how she had the qualities he wanted in a wife. He told her things she had been unaware of. For example, when she had gotten a flat tire at the entrance to the seminary, Emerson and a friend tried to change the tire, but they had the wrong tools. Emerson then called security and asked them to watch Dorcas's car. He told her about other similar situations that had been prompted by his love for her. He wanted to make sure she was safe and well taken care of, even when he was not present.

Emerson told Dorcas about his feelings for her, explaining that he knew she wasn't aware of them. "You don't need to return my feelings. I just wanted you to know how I feel," Emerson concluded.

Dorcas's response was less than encouraging. "Emerson, you are an excellent guy. You're kind, polite, personable. I would recommend you to any of my friends, but I don't have any romantic feelings for you. I have been praying since I came to Chicago to meet a lifetime partner."

Emerson was disappointed to say the least. Yet he valued Dorcas's friendship. He told her that he understood her trust in God to bring someone into her life.

9

POWER TO PRACTICE PATIENCE

"Love is patient" (1 Cor. 13:4).

In dating relationships, Dorcas had been very picky and demanding. She was known as a "high-maintenance" kind of girl. She only went out with the guys everybody else wanted. Her dates were for her to show off. But Dorcas found herself at the point in her life where she was no longer interested in dating for the fun of it. She wanted only friendship or a husband. She talked with her close friends about all of this and confided, "I'm serious now."

Even though Dorcas wasn't physically attracted to Emerson at first, as handsome as he is, she took the initiative to start a dating compromise. She recognized God's hand in Emerson's approach and manner; and she didn't want to hurt him, since he was a true friend. So, Dorcas and Emerson agreed to dating rules. After all, he did have the qualities she wanted in a husband.

Dorcas treated their relationship as a series of interviews in a marriage process. Emerson suffered a lot because of this. Dorcas hardly showed her feelings and responded little to his affection and care.

Emerson was the first guy Dorcas held hands with in public. She was fiercely independent and wouldn't run the risk of someone claiming any part of her, not even her hand. She felt like a wild horse free to enjoy any and everything she wanted. She had feared a boyfriend would hold her back and tie her down.

Their first date was disappointing for Emerson. Actually, it never happened. When Dorcas arrived to visit Emerson at seminary, she brought 3 friends with her. They spent all day together as a group. In the afternoon, Emerson asked Dorcas to go to the park with him. She agreed and invited everyone to join them. When they got back to the seminary, Emerson told Dorcas he was upset that they had not had their date. Their time together had not been special; in fact, they had not even had a date. Dorcas tried to explain. "It just didn't feel natural to leave my friends behind," she said. "It just wasn't natural. Why can't we be with other people?" Emerson dropped the discussion and Dorcas thought she had gotten away with her plan.

Emerson was disturbed all night. He barely slept. *What could Dorcas possibly be thinking and feeling*? he thought. *Her behavior has certainly not been natural.* And even if it were to be construed as such, it lacked integrity. Dorcas had said she was looking forward to their first date. She had written about how nice it would be. Their "date" had been anything but a date. So Emerson wrote a letter to Dorcas.

Perhaps Dorcas had won the battle, but Emerson wasn't giving up the war. In big letters with underlined words, as if he was shouting at her, Emerson wrote, "It's not natural to bring friends to a first date. It's not natural not to spend any time alone with your date. It's not natural to share every breathing moment of the day with a group of people. It's not natural to call a get-together of friends a date."

Later, Dorcas called Emerson and asked him to forgive her. She admitted to being afraid to be alone with him. "It's a big step for me to move from friendship to courtship," she explained.

During spring break, Emerson planned to visit Dorcas in Chicago. They had been invited to her cousin's house, where two other families were also invited to stay. One family were mutual friends from seminary and the other was their pastor from

Louisville. Emerson contacted both families ahead of time and asked them not to come during that week; and if they did, to give him and Dorcas time to be alone. When she found out about Emerson's calls and requests, Dorcas was furious! Both of these families had been extremely kind to Dorcas and had received her in their homes many times before. Both families and Emerson came to Chicago.

The visit went well. It was March and the spring air was filled with new life and new possibilities. Saturday turned into a wonderful day. Dorcas and Emerson enjoyed a spaghetti dinner at her apartment. Later, they shared their first kiss.

But not everything went so smoothly that week. While walking around the zoo with the pastor's family, Dorcas and Emerson held hands, causing the pastor to tease them. "What is this? Emerson and Dorcas have been holding hands and making eyes at each other all day," he said. "What do you suppose it means?" Dorcas was so embarrassed! She wished the earth would open up and swallow her. Later, however, once she was past being embarrassed and annoyed, Dorcas was no longer uncomfortable holding hands with Emerson in public.

In just a few short months, Emerson had learned a lot about Dorcas. While he already knew a lot about her spiritual qualities, he was also learning more about her personality. Dorcas was sure of herself, a natural-born leader, spontaneous, and quick-witted. She could wing just about any situation. She was gregarious and happy-go-lucky. She surely didn't feel a need to be married. She was responsible, stable, and fun to be around. She was always the leader of social action and had a constant need for adventure. Going to the park, enjoying family, taking trips, smelling the roses, swimming across river and upstream, Dorcas was always on the go. And one thing was obvious, Dorcas was always part of a group. If Dorcas was there, she would be accompanied by a host of people. Emerson realized that he would have to accept this openly and willingly if there was to be a relationship between them.

Another great date—for Dorcas—was a time when she took along not 3 people, but 35! She and the entire Hispanic mission from Chicago met Emerson at a Puerto Rican friend's house in Indiana. As if there weren't enough people on this supposed date, Dorcas also had arranged for the Hispanic mission in Kentucky to prepare the Saturday night meal for all of them. It was the first time Dorcas and Emerson stood as a couple in front of both churches.

On Sunday morning, when the Chicago pastor preached at St. Matthews Baptist Church Hispanic Mission, Dorcas received a surprise. Earlier she had mentioned to Emerson that he never did anything in public to express his feelings for her. So, ever quick to please, Emerson brought flowers and a card and presented them to Dorcas during the fellowship time following the Sunday service.

Summer was coming and Dorcas was planning for a great time. Recalling the fun summers in Puerto Rico as a child, she decided to go back for a visit; and, as usual, she didn't consider going alone. Dorcas invited just about everybody she knew, except Emerson. She didn't want to worry about him. She just wanted to enjoy her visit and have fun.

Doubts about her relationship with Emerson continued to plague Dorcas. He wanted her all to himself. He wanted time for a romantic courtship; intimate, soft-spoken conversations; a special bond apart from other friendships.

One day when Emerson was visiting in Chicago, a group of friends were at Dorcas's apartment. One of them turned to Emerson and asked if he was going with the group to Puerto Rico that summer. Dorcas overheard the question. When Emerson responded, "I haven't been invited," the air became thick with tension. Dorcas heard herself say, "Well, you can go if you want to." Not missing an opportunity, Emerson smiled and quickly accepted the forced invitation.

The trip to Puerto Rico worked out well. Dorcas went for two weeks. Her friends came the first week and Emerson came the second. When Aunt Mercedes and Aunt Lina met Emerson, they said, *"El mismo Manolo"* ("the same Manolo"). (They compared him to Dorcas's grandfather who was highly respected and loved by the whole family.) While this was a high compliment for Emerson, Dorcas feet pressured by it.

At the end of the second week, Dorcas and Emerson sat alone at a restaurant. As their conversation took on a serious note, Dorcas told Emerson that they probably wouldn't make good marriage material. She admitted to being loud and talkative, while he was quiet and reserved. She was afraid she would be domineering, and that wouldn't be right. With her outgoing nature, she felt she would be taking advantage of him.

Emerson listened patiently, then assured Dorcas that he did have strong opinions and would not back down on important issues. She wouldn't take advantage of him, he assured her. When something was important to him, she would know about it. Until now there hadn't been anything important to argue about. When the time came for Emerson to stand his ground, he would.

The couple continued to talk about marriage. As they left the restaurant, Emerson said, "You know you'll be missing out if you don't choose me as your mate." Dorcas childlike, hanging her head, responded, "I know."

The next day they went to Luquillo Beach, one of the most beautiful beaches in the world. Emerson was lost in thought and a bit depressed, thinking he and Dorcas would probably break up after all. *Maybe he was supposed to remain single*, he thought. He told Dorcas that if she turned him down, he would take it as a sign from God that he was to forget marriage and remain single.

After returning from vacation in Puerto Rico, Emerson continued to write letters and send audiotapes to Dorcas. But her doubts didn't subside. Dorcas talked to her father about her relationship with

Emerson and even allowed him to read some of Emerson's letters. Dorcas's father told her that she was the one who was sabotaging the relationship. Dorcas's family loved Emerson and already saw them as a couple. However, their friends did not see them that way.

As months went by, Dorcas and Emerson struggled to continue their relationship. They just didn't seem to mesh—they didn't fit each other well. One day Emerson called Dorcas and asked her to meet him at a restaurant to talk.

Emerson began the conversation. "Dorcas, we had an agreement to date and see if we were right for each other," he said. "I love you, but you haven't grown any. Would you like to call it off now?" Dorcas was surprised and upset. She responded by saying that if he was breaking up with her to say so, because she had no intentions of breaking up with him!

Emerson shook his head and continued. He didn't want to break up, but he simply hadn't seen any growth in their relationship. Dorcas argued. She had grown a lot. Maybe compared to other relationships he had experienced she was moving slowly. After all, it had only been a year. Dorcas reminded Emerson that, until he came along, she had never even held a guy's hand in public. She had never introduced anyone to her family and friends as a *boyfriend*. She had never before had the kind of relationship she had with him. It may seem that she hadn't grown, but she had.

Dorcas had given Emerson more of herself than she had ever given to one person. Just that week she had talked to Aunt Mercedes about his godly characteristics and his being the kind of man she would marry. "I can't tell you that I love you," Dorcas finally told Emerson, "but I am growing, and I don't want to break up."

The meeting had been difficult for Dorcas. She had made changes, but she remained unsure of romantic feelings for Emerson. Spiritually she had determined he was a good and godly choice for a mate.

After listening to Dorcas give evidence of her growth, Emerson still had little reassurance. After all, she still had not said she loved him.

10

POWER TO LOVE

"'The Lord does not look at the things man looks at. Man looks at the outward appearance, but the Lord looks at the heart'" (1 Sam. 16:7).

Shortly after Dorcas returned to Chicago, she heard a sermon titled, "David, a Man After God's Own Heart." In talking about why divorce is so prevalent, the preacher said, "Today people choose spouses based on outer appearance." People simply base their decisions for mates on variable external factors, he said. "What we should do is choose a mate based on godly characteristics and inner beauty. Is he or she personable? Do they show evidence of having the fruits of the Spirit? Do they have integrity? If you can answer yes to these questions, then your marriage will last a lifetime."

Dorcas heard this message as if it were straight from the lips of God. She realized she did love Emerson! *He is just like David*, she thought. As soon as the service was over, Dorcas found a telephone and called Emerson. "I love your insides, Emerson. I love you for who you are. I love you because you seek God in all you do." Words poured out of her mouth so fast Emerson hardly had time to absorb the message.

Dorcas loved him! She knew she loved him! She was actually telling him that she loved him! Without waiting for much response, Dorcas hung up and called her mother. "Mom, I love Emerson. I just called him and told him I love his insides."

Dorcas's mother was confused. "What do you mean? You called Emerson and told him you love his insides? What about his outside? You've been going out with him for a year, and you don't realize there is some physical attraction? How do you think it feels for someone to say they love your insides? What would you feel like if Emerson only told you he loves your insides? Dorcas, men are just like women. They need to know you appreciate all of them—inside and out. Call Emerson right now and tell him you love his outside; you love all of him."

For the second time that day, Emerson answered the phone to hear Dorcas's voice. "Emerson, I love your outside too. I love you—all of you. I love who you are and everything about you."

Finally, their love was established. *Maybe now*, Emerson thought, *we can enjoy a romantic courtship like other normal couples*. He would learn, though, that life with Dorcas is always an adventure, with twists and turns only God can foretell.

A few weeks after Dorcas had declared her love for Emerson came the interview with Union Baptist Association in Houston. She called Emerson to discuss the job with him and to ask him to pray about her decision. She felt there was a possibility that God was leading her to Houston. Emerson supported Dorcas and reassured her that God would supply him with a place to work and serve in Houston as easily as anywhere else. After all, he would be graduating in May and would have to look for work wherever they settled.

Dorcas's job opportunity directly affected their relationship. It certainly sped things up. At the end of a Thanksgiving family celebration in Orlando, Florida, Dorcas's mother's best friend, Toñita Carrion, gave Dorcas and Emerson a notebook with instructions to plan their wedding on the drive back to Louisville. Dorcas and Emerson were stunned, but followed her advice. Weddings did take a lot of planning, and this was one of the few times they would be together without interruptions for 15 hours.

Dorcas's ideal wedding involved celebrating with people from each church she had been a part of. She called various friends from all of these churches, asking one to arrange decorations and another to host a reception. She and Emerson would travel from Chicago to Louisville, to Orlando, to New Orleans, and of course to Puerto Rico and Guatemala to celebrate their marriage with their respective families and friends.

By the time they arrived back in Louisville, Dorcas and Emerson had planned only two wedding celebrations—one in Louisville and one in Puerto Rico—and a Thanksgiving service in Guatemala. Emerson was grateful that Dorcas had agreed to limit their celebrations to only three!

They agreed that both of their fathers would lead in the ceremony, and that all current and former pastors would participate as well. They wanted both English and Spanish to be used in all parts of the ceremony. The color scheme and music would be the similar at each wedding. And the wedding invitations instructed: *Go to the wedding nearest you.*

There would be some slight differences, however. The Louisville wedding would be held in the morning at St. Matthews Baptist Church with a breakfast reception following.

The bridal party there would be larger—ten bridesmaids, five groomsmen, two flower girls, and one wedding dress train carrier. Emerson would sing to Dorcas "I Will Be Here," and Dorcas would sing to Emerson "Only God Could Love You More."

The Puerto Rico wedding would take place in the afternoon. It would be more formal, with a dinner reception to follow at the Rotary Club. The bridal party would be smaller—five bridesmaids, two godparents, one flower girl, one ringbearer, and one wedding dress train carrier. Emerson and Dorcas would sing "Household of Faith" as a duet in Spanish.

The day Emerson went to buy rings for Dorcas was a terrible day. He had wanted her to pick out the rings she wanted. That, to her, was culturally unacceptable. So, Emerson enlisted a friend to shop with him. The men felt inadequate for such an important job. But Dorcas had assured Emerson that whatever ring he put on her finger she would love and cherish forever.

Emerson couldn't shake his insecurity. *What if she didn't like it? What if it didn't look good on her?* Finally, he saw a diamond solitaire similar to his mother's. It was perfect, but now he had to find the wedding band. He begged Dorcas to help choose it, but she refused. Emerson had to choose one on his own.

Emerson and Dorcas spent Christmas with his parents. When his family met Dorcas, they instantly accepted her as a part of the family. Dorcas expected Emerson to give her the engagement ring for Christmas; instead, he gave her a portrait he had drawn of her. She was a bit disappointed, but the drawing was beautiful.

New Year's Eve was one of those rare, carefully orchestrated moments in which Emerson and Dorcas were alone. He chose this time to give Dorcas her ring. He knew it would be a special, intimate moment they would both cherish in their memory. He also wanted the expression to symbolize a new year and a new life together.

The ring was absolutely beautiful: a half-carat diamond solitaire and a matching band with two small diamonds and two rubies. Dorcas was so happy. She proudly put on this symbol of a new life together.

Both weddings were wonderful and all Dorcas dreamed they would be. After their second wedding in Puerto Rico, Dorcas and Emerson spent their first night together. Then both sets of parents drove the newlyweds to the airport for their honeymoon in Guatemala.

Dorcas's mother teased her. "Mrs. Byrd, you are no longer a *señorita*," she said. "Now, you are Mrs. Byrd, no longer a child. Now you are a woman, Mrs. Byrd." Dorcas was embarrassed, but she had kept a solemn commitment of purity and holiness to God. She had dealt with her peers teasing and taunting her about her decision; but to Dorcas, this was a serious matter. She had kept her promise to remain a virgin until marriage.

Dorcas had never been to Guatemala and Emerson wanted to make sure she enjoyed this trip. He made reservations at the luxurious Hotel Antigua Guatemala. It was filled with tropical vegetation, flowers, and plants everywhere in every imaginable color. Parrots and parakeets were in trees and cages inside and outside the hotel. The hotel itself was lovely, with parquet floors, dark mahogany wood furnishings, and bright tapestries. Dorcas had never seen such a beautiful hotel.

Monday through Wednesday Dorcas prepared at the poolside for her assignments at the National Acteens Convention (NAC), which closely followed their wedding. Thursday Emerson's parents took them to lunch at Posada Don Rodrigo, where marimba music filled the air. The restaurant held wonderful memories for

Emerson. He had eaten there for special occasions when he was a child. *How could he possibly convey and share with Dorcas all this place meant to him?*

On Friday night, the Guatemalan mission family had a wedding shower for Dorcas and Emerson. They wanted to be sure Emerson had all the typical items that would keep Guatemala close to his heart. They showered the couple with brightly colored shirts, tablecloths and napkins, and wooden objects such as a gorgeous tray of fruit and a spice rack with wooden jars.

Saturday morning Dorcas, Emerson, and his family went to a high school graduation ceremony for Katrina, one of the MKs, at Hotel Antigua Guatemala. That afternoon the couple celebrated their marriage at a Thanksgiving service at Guatemalan Baptist Seminary.

The celebration was similar to a wedding, with Emerson and Dorcas giving their testimonies about how God had brought them together and what they would do in Houston working at the Baptist Mission Centers. Their Guatemalan godparents, missionaries Ted and Sue Lindwall, prayed for them and blessed them. Emerson and Dorcas sang "Household of Faith" as a duet in Spanish. There was special music, ushers, flowers—a big to-do. Emerson wore a suit and Dorcas wore her white street-length going away outfit. A tamale reception, and of course a wedding cake, followed the celebration.

During this memorable honeymoon trip, Dorcas met most of Emerson's childhood friends. He was glad to be able to share good childhood memories with his new wife. One of the side trips they took was to Panajachel, where Emerson had spent a week every year at the annual Mission meeting. When the couple checked in at the Cacique Inn, Doña Adelita, the owner, recognized Emerson and gave the couple a complimentary stay.

11

POWER TO LET GO

"For the foolishness of God is wiser than man's wisdom, and the weakness of God is stronger than man's strength" (1 Cor. 1:25).

In April 1994, a month before her weddings, Dorcas moved to Houston to begin her new ministry. She became totally submerged in the work at the Houston Baptist Mission Centers, directing activities of the volunteers, receiving donations, distributing clothes and food, and learning all the aspects of running the centers. The demands of her job took all of Dorcas's time and energy.

After the weddings in May, Emerson also moved to Houston and began volunteering full-time at the Baptist Mission Centers while he looked for a job. Dorcas was thankful and appreciative of Emerson's help. He always seemed to be in the right place at the right time and knew exactly what to do. Even with his assistance, the work was demanding and stressful. It was almost a year before Emerson found a job because of all the time he spent in the centers.

Volunteers prepared and ordered materials and supplies for just about everything. The directors of the centers checked on the facilities, but rarely made suggestions for maintenance or improvement. To Dorcas it seemed that everyone was focused on surviving, just getting through the day. There seemed to be little thought about the future, no vision.

Dorcas began to become more involved in matching people with particular ministries and asked them to report to her. She also provided additional supervisory training for the directors of the individual centers and asked them to supply her with maintenance needs reports, attendance reports, and the projected number of volunteers they needed for specific tasks. She also requested from them reports of transformed lives.

Dorcas appointed assistant directors for each ministry to give the directors more time to supervise, report, project, and tell the stories. For the centers, she created an organizational chart, posted the chart at the centers, and distributed copies. Volunteers began to have more direction for their work. They knew to whom to report for which ministries.

While the organizational plan did not eliminate all the stress, it did help smooth things out. Dorcas also enlisted her family's support. Some people responded by praying and giving, while others actually moved to Houston to help in a more direct way. Dorcas's aunts who were there for her physical birth, who guided and taught her through childhood, adolescence, and early adulthood, also assisted in birthing her into full-time Christian ministry. The aunts' commitment to Christ and family only gained in strength as they matured and aged.

Aunt Lina, already in her 70s, and Aunt Mercedes came to help Dorcas start her work at the Baptist Mission Centers. They worked in the centers every day and prepared dinner for Dorcas and Emerson every night.

Aunt Mercedes gave Dorcas ideas for improvement based on her excellent organizational skills. Aunt Lina had a special talent in making lesson plans for preschoolers and for interacting with them. The children loved her. So, Aunt Lina worked with the children, while Aunt Mercedes helped Dorcas hone her leadership and organizational skills. One of Aunt Mercedes's major projects was organizing the clothing ministry.

When, after a year of living in Houston, Aunt Mercedes returned to Puerto Rico, Aunt Lina chose to stay in Houston. However, she could not afford to live on her own. This created a wonderful opportunity for Aunt Lina to live with Emerson and Dorcas. She designed her own curriculum for the children she taught at the centers.

On the weekend before Labor Day, Dorcas's mother's family had a reunion in Orlando, Florida. This was a grand event, with so many family members being able to attend. Dorcas, Emerson, and Aunt Lina drove all the way from Houston to Orlando in 18 hours. On the trip home, Aunt Lina talked about how satisfied she was with her life now that she had organized and structured a program for the 2- and 3-year-olds. She said, "I can die happy now. I have accomplished my number one dream in life."

On Sunday of the following weekend, Aunt Lina woke up feeling bad. She thought about going to the hospital, but she did not want to get in the way of the Lord's work or interfere with the scheduled activities of the day. Dorcas's relatives and friends had come to help with special Labor Day weekend activities. Many of her cousins were there, as well as friends Patti Villarreal and Adam Castro.

Emerson saw how sick Aunt Lina was and wanted to take her to the hospital, but Aunt Lina refused to interrupt the day's activities. She insisted on staying home.

When the family came home after the worship service to check on Aunt Lina, she said she was feeling fine. That afternoon, Aunt Lina stayed home to rest more while everybody else went to the Astrodome for a baseball game and a community worship service afterward. Aunt Lina knew that the activities would last a long time and she would be too tired to enjoy the worship service.

During the afternoon, Dorcas called from her office to check on Aunt Lina. "I'm doing just fine. You all enjoy and take care," Aunt Lina assured Dorcas. Everyone enjoyed the baseball game, and later the sermon touched the hearts of many people.

Dorcas and her family got home late that evening. When they arrived, Aunt Lina appeared to be asleep. Everyone was quiet so they would not to disturb her. Dorcas noticed that Aunt Lina was sitting peacefully in the formal living room, which was unusual for her. She had always gone to her room when she was ready to sleep and did not stay up waiting for others to come home. Dorcas understood what the others could not. She screamed and began crying and sobbing.

As if chained to the ground, Dorcas stood shaking, trembling, and calling Aunt Lina's name. Family members checked on Aunt Lina because she had not moved despite Dorcas's screaming. Aunt Lina was dead.

Doctors told Dorcas that her aunt had died quietly. She apparently had a heart attack and died quickly, with little pain, about an hour before the family had come home.

Emerson called relatives and answered the phone as Dorcas cried through the night. Dorcas was devastated. Aunt Lina would never hold or teach her children. Dorcas's children would never know the genuine joy that radiated from Aunt Lina. The memory of Aunt Lina would always be with Dorcas, and she would share that memory with her children.

Aunt Lina's funeral was on Wednesday. An important board meeting was canceled, as were all the centers' activities. Volunteers, center staff members, and ministers alike came to support Dorcas through her grief. Most of them knew Aunt Lina well. Their presence comforted Dorcas and helped healing to begin. Dorcas cried on the shoulders of countless caring friends and talked to them about her beloved aunt.

This was Dorcas's first experience with death of a loved one. Although she could not understand why God had chosen to take Aunt Lina away from her, she felt God's strength. Later she came to realize how gracious God had been with her in this experience. He had allowed her to have beautiful last words with Aunt Lina. He had allowed her to live with Dorcas and Emerson in their home. He had allowed her to have so many Christians surround her and immerse her with their love in Jesus' name.

12

POWER TO EMPOWER OTHERS

"Do not merely listen to the word, and so deceive yourselves. Do what it says" (James 1:22).

Just a few weeks after their weddings, Emerson and Dorcas participated on the program at the National Acteens Convention (NAC) held in Birmingham, Alabama. They were excited to speak about their new ministry and the work at Houston's Baptist Mission Centers. Dorcas was excited to be among so many committed teenagers, but the intensity of the meetings was exhausting. It dawned on Dorcas that she was no longer a teenager, although she felt like it had been such a short time since she had been. The best part of NAC for Dorcas was seeing the results later that summer in the form of an Acteens Activators team and a Sojourner.*

This was Dorcas's first summer at the centers, and she was grateful that volunteer missions groups—mostly high school students—from all over the United States, as well as about two dozen Sojourners and a dozen summer missionaries (college student volunteers), had come to help. She was particularly proud of a group of Acteens from Arkansas because she had participated in their commissioning service earlier. All the volunteers were assigned through the Home Mission Board (now North American Mission Board) for various lengths of time.

The four centers were full of activity during Dorcas's first summer. Volunteer groups came in for a week at a time to do construction work, park ministries, weeklong kids clubs, twice-a-week teen clubs, crafts, repairs on mission facilities and neighborhood houses, cleanup, sorting and organizing of donated clothes, stocking of the food pantry, and food distribution. They also provided special music and testimonies for worship services, led Bible studies, helped prepare food for special events, and participated in other tasks as needed.

Both Sojourners and summer missionaries, affectionately called "critters," live at one of the Baptist Mission Centers for the duration of the time they serve. Most stay for six, eight, or ten weeks, weeks that change not only the lives of those with whom they work but their lives as well.

Local Houston churches provide three meals a day all summer for the critters. On Sundays the critters visit in local churches, sharing their testimonies and speaking about the Baptist Mission Centers. Their enthusiasm and energy are contagious and motivate local church members to donate time to the centers on a more regular basis, all year round.

By the end of the summer, many critters decide to become involved in full-time ministry and missions. They return to their homes, consciously making decisions that keep them focused on and committed to ministry and missions.

Jan Griggs served as a semester missionary at the Houston Baptist Mission Centers. She states what so many find true, "I have been learning about missions all my life, from Mission Friends® through Girls in Action® and Acteens®. I am so thankful that I was brought up in a Christian home and church that taught me about my responsibility to tell others. I have always loved learning about missions; now I love learning from missions!"

Amanda Nicole Parmley, a Sojourner from the Liberal Arts Academy at Johnston High School in Austin, Texas, refers to her stay as the "best ten weeks of my life." She lived and worked beside 36 other critters. Each day the group divided into teams and went to the centers. Her favorite activity was Kids Club. Neighborhood children came to play outside, make crafts, sing songs, and participate in a special event on Fridays. During the week there were opportunities for the critters to share their faith in Christ with all the children.

One day as they were playing outside, Amanda overheard 4-year-old Mario singing: "Thank You, God, for little worms. Thank You, God." Her heart skipped a beat as she realized that the preschoolers were actually learning and absorbing everything she taught them in class. God spoke to her through this and many other occasions during those ten weeks. His message was loud and clear: "I use ordinary people to do extraordinary things. What I want with you is a close personal relationship. It is my Holy Spirit in you that makes you exceptional."

By the end of her stay, Amanda knew that her actions in her ordinary daily life were what would draw people to Christ or push them away. She had also committed to obeying God, no matter how simple or distasteful the task, so that He could draw people unto Himself.

Jan Griggs arrived at the center during a crisis time. A family of six children had been participating in Kids Club, Teen Club, and various other center activities. Suddenly, the children's father died, leaving them without parental guidance. Only the oldest, Edgar, was attending school; and because of his father's illness and death, he had missed two weeks of school. Jan helped him every day, after her regular work, to catch up with his school assignments. One of his assignments was to read *To Kill a Mockingbird*. He found the novel hard to understand, so Jan read it to him. Being from the South made it easy for her to explain the expressions and terms that Edgar did not quite understand. Jan also worked with the local schools to complete the necessary paperwork to enroll the other children in school.

Of those six children, only José has not accepted Christ. José was 15 when Jan met him. He was a teenager full of anger and bitterness. He used drugs to try to handle difficult situations, creating a deep, dark, vicious cycle. One day he stole a car and drove to his home. Because his 14-year-old brother, Irán, was also at home when the police came, both boys were arrested. They served two days of detention before receiving probation. José broke the conditions of probation by not going to school. Irán went to school for three days, then dropped out. The children had moved four times between January and May and all the children quit going to school.

Irán went back to jail for breaking probation. Jan visited and read the Bible with him every day. Before he got out of jail, Irán was participating in Bible study and confessed to doing wrong. He committed himself to God, the courts, and the school. He became known as "Bible Boy" and led his cell mate to become a Christian. His favorite passage was Jeremiah 29:11–13: "'For I know the plans I have for you,' declares the Lord, 'plans to prosper you and not to harm you, plans to give you hope and a future. Then you will call upon me and come and pray to me, and I will listen to you. You will seek me and find me when you seek me with all your heart.'"

When the time came for Irán's court appearance, he and Jan trusted God with the court's decision for his life and future. Jan testified on his behalf, and Irán knew that God knew his heart. God could see how his heart had changed. Irán was confident that God would send him home, and He did. Irán is thankful to God for sending Jan to minister to him.

José was also arrested for breaking probation. He continued doing drugs and participating in gang activity. Jan visited him also until the court sentenced him to a two-year program, three hours away. Jan continues to write to him and prays he will open his heart and accept God's love.

Jan says, "These people here at the Baptist centers often barely have enough to get by, but they still open their hearts and homes to help others. It warms my heart to see such love and loyalty in a world where the two are so seldom found."

Jan also worked closely with another family with four children. Although they lived in a crowded little house, when an aunt faced tough financial problems, the family made room for her and her four children to live with them.

The family is daily learning more about love—God's love. They are a prime example of how powerful prayer can be. Three of the children attend Teen Club at Fletcher and Gano centers and have all become Christians. The 14-year-old son developed a burden for his parents. His father was an alcoholic, and the parents fought with each other constantly. He began to pray that his parents would accept Christ and that God would restore his family. Day after day at Teen Club, he requested prayer for his parents. Night after night, he read his Bible and prayed for God to reach them.

After many months and many prayers by the children, the missionaries, pastors, and others, the mother too decided to become a Christian. Later, the family welcomed a visit from Gano Mission Center director María Tobias and her husband, Reverend Pedro Tobias. After listening to María and Pedro, the father also accepted Christ as his personal Savior. The entire family is now active in a local Southern Baptist church. As a family, they are growing closer to each other as a result of growing closer to God.

Volunteers like Jan Griggs, Amanda Nicole Parmley, and the scores of youth groups and other missions teams are an integral part of the ministry of the Baptist Mission Centers. Sheila Bowden, another semester missionary, agrees with many of her fellow volunteers. "I have learned so much from my co-workers and from the people in the community. I know my life will never be the same."

The powerful bank of volunteers allows the centers to offer a wide variety of ministries. And by offering so many different ministries, the staff and volunteers can meet a variety of needs. The work can be very tiring. Angela Pennington, another semester missionary, says, "Day-to-day activities can become routine unless I keep my personal relationship with Christ as top priority. When you are in good spiritual shape, you see every day as an opportunity waiting to be taken. The kids here need love. How could I claim to be a Christian and say I feel too tired or I do not have enough time to reach out to them?"

---

*Acteens Activators is a short-term volunteer missions program for Acteens and their advisors or adult leaders. Sojourners is a program which allows high school graduates to assist in missions for a summer or a year. Rising high school seniors may serve as Sojourners for the summer.

13

POWER THROUGH PRAYER

"Blessed is the man who does not walk in the counsel of the wicked or stand in the way of sinners or sit in the seat of mockers. But his delight is in the law of the Lord, and on his law he meditates day and night" (Psalm 1:1–2).

In the midst of sharing in the experiences of the staff and volunteers, Dorcas must deal with harsh realities. She leans heavily on her personal relationship with God, continually meditating in His Word.

One morning Dorcas's supervisor, Tom Billings, called to tell her that the centers were in financial distress. Already overwhelmed by her daily administrative tasks and decisions, this news was just too much for Dorcas to bear. She wanted to quit. She was mad at God for bringing her to Houston. She missed the direct, one-on-one contact with people that she had at her job in Chicago. *Why has God brought me here just to waste my talents?* she thought. *I can't use my people gifts effectively in this job.* What this job needed was what she had the least of—administrative gifts.

Dorcas felt she wasn't part of anything useful. It seemed all her time was consumed in the organization itself, board meetings, and other office duties. *Wasn't there someone else who could do some of this work?* she questioned. After all, these centers were running when Dorcas arrived. Why must she make all the decisions?

After listening to her boss talk about the financial state of the centers, Dorcas thought about calling an emergency board meeting. The budget problem—a weighty one—weighed heavily on Dorcas's mind. Dorcas knew that money problems don't wait, they just get worse. The centers were $19,000 in debt.

At that time, Christine McDonald, Dorcas's secretary, had been reading a book about a ministry based entirely on prayer. Whenever they had a need, they would bring the need to the people and pray as a group. Christine boldly told Dorcas, "We don't need an emergency board meeting. We need an emergency prayer meeting!" Dorcas immediately seized the idea. She could not deal with the budget problem; only God could take care of it. Dorcas responded, "That's right. Let's pray tonight at 7:00." A short memo went out to all staff and volunteers: "Mandatory prayer meeting tonight at 7:00."

After an hour of praying individually, in small groups, and corporately, a sense of revival filled the room. They felt a peace about the situation. God would provide. And, He certainly did.

One of the volunteers who had worked earlier in the day told Dorcas that he had something in his truck to give to her. "You gather the staff and volunteers while I go get it," he requested. When the man came back, he handed her $1,000. "God told me to bring money today," he said. "I wasn't sure for what, but the impression was so strong I went to the bank and took it out. Now I know why."

On the spot, the group offered a prayer of thanksgiving. Before Dorcas could leave, another volunteer gave her a check for $1,000 and requested to remain anonymous. Dorcas couldn't help thinking what might have happened had they prayed for more than an hour!

Days later, Dorcas spoke at a church service and told about the prayer meeting. After she spoke, the pastor asked Dorcas and Emerson to come to the front. The pastor addressed the congregation: "We

are in a building project for a new sanctu-
ary, but I feel compelled to have a special
collection. Give what's on your hearts."
The offering totaled $2,000. Again Dorcas
was in awe of how God provides.

Dorcas's first year at the centers ended
with all bills paid and some money in the
bank. In retrospect it had been a good
year. God had provided above and
beyond Dorcas's expectations. She looked
forward to a new year with fewer ups and
downs. Having Emerson at her side for
the past six months had been especially
pleasant, both at work and at home.

Emerson and Dorcas went to Puerto
Rico to lead conferences at the annual
church and community ministries confer-
ence in March 1995. They talked about
the importance of participating in a variety of ministries and volunteer service
and helped train 64 people for volunteer
service. They complemented each other
so well, it was nice to work together. She
would miss him when he found a job and
went to work elsewhere in Houston.

In April, Emerson accepted a job as a
youth counselor for nearby Montgomery
County. He was able to use and sharpen
skills he had acquired during seminary.
This job also gave him an opportunity to
get his license as a clinical social worker.

As the months went by, Dorcas and the other workers prayed for God to send someone to take on the enormous task of maintenance. In October the centers decided to have a Missions Expo. They invited all the churches in the Union Baptist Association, providing booths for each ministry. The program included a presentation of the centers and a request for more volunteers. One of the people who responded was Tom Turner. He said, "I have just retired, and I'd like to take over the maintenance for the centers. But you must give me total control over maintenance decisions." Dorcas almost burst for joy. The Lord had heard her plea! Quickly she grasped his hand in a firm handshake and said, "OK, that's a deal."

Although Tom found a virtually nonexistent budget for maintenance, that did not stop him. He had things looking good in no time. He donated $4,000 for this ministry through his church; and within a few months, everything was up to par and only required regular upkeep.

Two other key positions remained unfilled in the organization. They needed a logistics manager to pick up and deliver furniture, food, and clothing, and an operational manager to keep the daily books and write checks for everyday activities and events. A retired accountant, Percy McCain, agreed to do both jobs.

Now with all the positions filled and a functioning organization in place, Dorcas had more time to speak in churches. However, staff concerns took up much of her time. She began to see herself in the role of vision setter, supervisor of personnel, program evaluator, and conflict manager.

The centers still had no financial plan, and a new financial crisis arose. This time, they were $14,000 in the hole. Dorcas relived a nightmare, thinking the centers would go under. More anxious than ever before, Dorcas called a few churches to pray and received a gift of $10,000 from one church. God had provided again in a major way.

Dorcas learned a new lesson. God will intervene. His work will be done and He will provide the resources. God told Dorcas, "These centers are Mine. I'm responsible. You have no control over them. You are to be a faithful servant, coordinating the volunteers and needs and telling churches what the needs are."

Dorcas felt another burden—those who received help rarely gave back to the community. They lacked a sense of servanthood. Adult Hispanics came for food, clothing, and English-as-a-second-language

(ESL) classes. Children and teenagers used the gym and other resources. Dorcas thought of a way for these people to learn the Christian and civic responsibility of giving to others, a way to help Christians demonstrate a Christlike life. As volunteers discipled new converts, they instructed the new converts to be part of a local church, to be servants in their communities, and to be like missionaries in the inner city.

During the second year, Dorcas adjusted and grew in her position. She saw a need to set strategic planning for the future of the centers. She approached the Baptist Mission Centers' Board of Directors and together they began planning the purpose of each center.

The Baptist Mission Centers as a whole exist to partner with local congregations in fulfilling the Great Commission by transforming broken communities in the Houston area. Fifteen avenues of ministry were established to help fulfill this purpose. Each ministry is designed to transform lives by introducing individuals to the life-changing power of a personal relationship with Jesus Christ, guiding members of the community to a Christlike approach to everyday problem solving, helping families become stronger and more independent, and encouraging families to become involved in local churches and in their communities.

Dorcas believes that the only way the centers can transform each community from hopelessness and fear to the richest of God's blessings is to introduce each person, one by one, to the Savior. "I know that if we could just disciple them and teach them more about Christ, other problems and concerns would lessen," she says.

Dorcas and the board of directors also have further refined the schedule of services to get the best use out of each property. For example, the Gano Center didn't have adequate child-care facilities, so they agreed to offer children's programs at the other centers. They developed other program schedules, all of which needed money. But as Dorcas had learned, God always provides the resources. A church called to offer money and volunteers for any renovation needed for the centers to accommodate the new program schedules.

The Food Bank, a local regulatory entity, approached Dorcas about the food ministry at the centers. It has strict regulations that food donors such as the centers must follow. They were concerned that the centers had wooden pallets on the ground and unclean storage areas, and that food recipients had no choice as to the foods they received. The Food Bank had observed that some recipients threw food on the street as they left the distribution center. They asked if Dorcas had a plan for improvement. She was able to reply, "Yes, of course. We're waiting on resources."

That same week Sandy Chance interviewed to be a volunteer. She had no idea of what to do. With tears in her eyes she said, "I don't want to do office work. I want to help start something new with the people."

Dorcas told her about the Food Bank concerns. She asked Sandy to go with her to a meeting with the Food Bank to determine the needs and requirements. Sandy was interested in the project and quickly agreed.

The Food Bank recommended that Dorcas and her staff use First Baptist Church, Pasadena, Texas, as a model for their distribution plan. Tom, Sandy, and Dorcas visited the church. The distribution center was not only clean but beautiful. People signed in, were interviewed one-on-one, chose the food items they needed, and waited. Volunteers prepared food bags from the immaculate "grocery store" and stapled to the bags a ticket with the person's name and list of food items included.

Tom said a program like this would cost about $26,000 to set up at Gano, just one of the centers. Downcast, Dorcas and Sandy gathered the paperwork they had been given and prepared to leave. Everything, everywhere involved more money than they could possibly imagine obtaining. And at this same time, along with Baptist Mission Centers concerns, Dorcas had just learned she was pregnant!

Back in Houston, Dorcas and Sandy met to decide how they could apply at least a few of the new methods they had seen at First Baptist Church, Pasadena. The women decided that Dorcas should talk to the board about simulating the Pasadena ministry. She asked about approaching the church that had offered to support new programming schedules. The board agreed. Asking couldn't possibly hurt, even though it seemed unlikely for any one church to be able and willing to finance such a commitment

Tom Turner, Dorcas, and board chairman Bob Newell went to the church and presented the future of the Baptist Mission Centers, the new food distribution program, and the costs. The church immediately gave them $16,000 and promised the balance by the summer. Tom, Bob, and Dorcas looked at each other in utter amazement. Once again, God had shown Dorcas it was His work.

And she was a faithful servant.

Those same words from God came again when Dorcas was asked to speak later at both the WMU Annual Meeting and the Southern Baptist Convention annual meeting in Atlanta, Georgia. She was in awe that He would give her that opportunity so early in life.

14

POWER TO SEIZE OPPORTUNITIES

"Humble yourselves before the Lord, and He will lift you up" (James 4:10).

Dorcas grew up admiring Woman's Missionary Union (WMU) leaders and speakers, but it never crossed her mind that she might become one of them. She had met Dellanna O'Brien, the national WMU executive director, when O'Brien toured Cook County Hospital in 1993.

WMU leaders had asked Dorcas to speak at their annual meeting about the Baptist Mission Centers in Houston and what God was doing there. The following Tuesday, she had been asked to give a three- to four-minute testimony during the Southern Baptist Convention. Remembering that week, Dorcas says, "How special that God would allow me to do this!"

Even after years of being a Christian, Dorcas stands amazed at the power of God. He provides opportunities to share our understanding, to humble ourselves, to be willing servants. Dorcas says, "My principal skills are encouraging, showing joy, and exalting Christ. Prayer has been the avenue for the results to come about."

While prayer has always been a vital part of Dorcas's relationship with God and with fellow Christians, she has learned that God answers our prayers in a variety of ways, often in ways we would never imagine possible. And often He uses people as answers to the prayers of others.

Such was the case in the lives of Jenny and Alfredo Rivas. While visiting with these dear friends in Chicago, Dorcas told the couple about the Baptist Mission Centers in Houston.

Jenny and Alfredo were so moved they said they would like to sell everything and move to Houston to do missions work at the centers. Dorcas could barely believe her ears. Jenny and Alfredo both had good careers. They had three children and a beautiful five-bedroom house. *How could they possibly come and be happy?* thought Dorcas. So, she suggested a short-term volunteer missions trip first.

In spring 1996, Alfredo visited for a week to see the work going on and to videotape it for Jenny. After he returned home and talked with Jenny and the children about all he had seen, the family made its decision. Alfredo and Jenny would sell everything, quit their jobs, and move the family to Houston. By June the Rivas family had arrived, ready for work.

For the first few months they lived in the apartment with Dorcas and Emerson. Alfredo immediately went to work on the house next door to the Joy Center, getting it ready for his family to move in. Jenny accepted the position of assistant director of the Joy Center, where she leads Wednesday Bible study classes, ministers to the children in Kids Club, and helps with other needs as they arise.

Alfredo is known as the Billy Graham of the neighborhood. Everybody knows and loves him, even those who are not Christians. On Tuesday nights, he works with older teenaged boys playing basketball. He also picks up food donations and organizes worship services at the Joy Center.

One volunteer group from Merritt Island, Florida, comes to Houston every year to spend a week. They were in Houston when Dorcas began her job there. Her first assignment for them was to clean out the linen closet, a closet that no one had dared to open. It was the kind of closet cartoons are made about, where the linens attack the person who opens the door. The volunteers waded through the towels and sheets as they categorized and labeled everything, right down to buttons and zippers. This volunteer group also installed a telephone system and bought all the necessary equipment for it. They continue to come every April to help Dorcas prepare for the other volunteer missions groups which arrive in June.

In summer 1996, volunteer missions groups started the construction for the new food distribution center. Contractors did specialized work that the volunteer groups could not do; and by the end of the summer, the new grocery store was a reality. In addition to the food distribution area, it features interview rooms and a waiting room.

Churches in the Houston area eagerly support Dorcas not only in her work but also in her brave decision to become a mother while directing the work of the Baptist Mission Centers. Churches, WMU groups, and two GA camps gave showers for "Baby Byrd." Champion Forrest Church hosted a Christmas in August for the baby. Cornerstone Baptist Church bought boxes of diapers and baby food. Dorcas's office was adapted so that she could take the baby to work. God provided resources through Christians supporting

Dorcas's ministry, and the baby was welcomed into a family of faith and ministry to people in the inner city. Dorcas cherishes this memory of being surrounded by God's love through His people.

Dorcas was eight months pregnant when the fall semester of programs at the centers began. Staff and volunteers were trained for the new food ministry and new program schedule at the Gano Center in August. Because of its excellent facilities, the Fletcher Center was chosen to house the clothing ministry, along with ESL classes, citizenship classes, and child care. The staff was divided among the four locations. The Gano and Fletcher centers piloted the new schedules. The other two centers kept the old schedule. Gano and Fletcher centers hosted Kids Club and Teen Club while the Joy and Gano centers offered Tae Kwon Do classes. Dorcas and her staff agreed to evaluate the new schedules at the end of the semester.

The fall 1996 programs got off to a roaring start. Plans fell smoothly into place, and the new schedules worked out as planned. In addition to the anticipated flurry of activity, an unusual opportunity came along. A church contacted the Baptist Mission Centers, wanting to buy the Mason Drive Mission Center. At first, the

Baptist Mission Centers' Board of Directors was concerned about how they could continue ministries to that community without operating that center. After some thought, they concluded that a church could minister to the community just as well as they could. The property was sold for $100,000. The ministries and volunteers from the Mason Drive Center merged with those at the Joy Center about a mile down the street.

Part of the money from the sale of the Mason Drive Center was used for repairs on the other centers. The rest was invested. These improvements allowed the Joy Center to have a simulated grocery store, clothing ministry, and educational ministry. The new vision for the Joy Center combined the ministries of both the Fletcher and Gano centers.

Another strong program that emerged for the Baptist Mission Centers was Urban Allies, a group of churches united in their efforts to support inner-city work by providing financial resources, volunteers, and prayer support. Representatives from Urban Allies meet monthly with Baptist Mission Centers staff. They receive a report and plan ways to provide for the next month's needs. Urban Allies pick up where the associational budget leaves off.

The biggest blessing of all for Dorcas that year was Abigail Jean, born September 25, 1996. When Dorcas returned to work six weeks later, she realized how difficult it had been for the Mason Drive and Joy centers' staffs to adjust to combined ministries. As a result, she made a new organizational plan and developed new job assignments for everyone.

Today, the Fletcher Baptist Mission Center has a mission home for four female missionaries, a gym, and a kitchen. It is staffed by a director, an assistant, a Mission Service Corps volunteer, a semester missionary, and several other volunteers. It offers children's classes, English-as-a-second-language (ESL) classes, citizenship and literacy classes, and a clothing ministry.

Ruth, the Fletcher Center's director, finds Dorcas a fun and wise person to work with. At first, Ruth sought Dorcas's advice for what to do in every situation. Dorcas responded to Ruth's numerous questions by asking her, "What would you do if I were not here?" Dorcas was quick to affirm Ruth's suggestions, saying, "Anytime you come to me with a problem, be ready to offer me a solution. You have more experience than I do. Share your knowledge with me." The Fletcher Center runs smoothly under Ruth's direction.

The Gano Baptist Mission Center operates under the direction of María Tobias. In 1994 Reverend Pedro Tobias asked Emerson to speak at his church. Before the meeting, Dorcas, Emerson, Pedro, and María (Pedro's wife) met to pray. When María, who is bilingual, learned about the ministry at Gano Center, she took a part-time position there as assistant director. A year later she agreed to be the full-time director. María says, "Fruit is coming out of the mission centers. We see people's material needs, but they are crying inside with spiritual needs as well." Pedro also became involved in the work of the center. First he came to preach, then he began to help with the ministry to senior adults, people like Abraham and Irene López.

Abraham was a good man, according to his wife. He provided for his family of 11 children and took care of her. Even after they were all adults, Abraham helped his children and grandchildren. But he also drank and led his own life on the side.

Then Abraham and Irene began attending Senior Adult Day at the Gano Center. Pedro took an interest in the couple and visited in their home. Over time he developed a relationship with them and ministered to them. As a result, Abraham and Irene both became Christians and now volunteer at the

Gano Baptist Mission Center.

In summer 1995, Barbara McCain, a volunteer, started visiting homebound people living in the area near the Gano Center. Many had terrible living conditions. Their houses needed repair, and many needed help with obtaining food and medical care. As Barbara reached out to them, she felt a burden for other senior adults. She instituted a luncheon program for the senior adults who were able to attend a time of fellowship and worship.

The death of a community resident, Mrs. Handkamer, led to an ongoing program for senior adults. Years earlier, Mrs. Handkamer had given the Baptist Mission Centers a grant from her foundation for senior programs, but no one on the Baptist Mission Centers' Board of Directors was aware of this generous gift. The grant had been suspended several years before for the lack of seniors-only programs. When a board member sent a sympathy card and letter to the family offering condolences, the Handkamer Foundation contacted the Baptist Mission Centers and asked if there was a senior adult program yet. Barbara was thrilled to provide the foundation with a report.

She had worked hard to develop the senior adult program without knowing about the suspended grant. Barbara had photographs of the summer luncheons and stories to accompany the photographs. She went personally to make the presentation to the foundation.

After the presentation, the foundation contacted Barbara to say they would fund the program with $30,000. Barbara immediately went to work on developing a full-fledged program, using the money to assist senior adults in obtaining refrigerators, fans, stoves, and air conditioners; and, of course, to support the weekly fellowship luncheons. Combining physical and spiritual growth has been a successful plan used by the Baptist Mission Centers. At their weekly Senior Adult Day, senior adults participate in classes designed to help them stay physically fit. They also exercise their minds by doing crafts and participating in Bible studies and prayer.

The program grew quickly. In 1996 a representative of the foundation came to videotape some of the activities. As a result, this program of the Gano Center received another grant for $50,000.

By 1997, there were about 150 senior adults attending the Thursday luncheon and Bible study. There are two senior adult groups, an English-speaking African-American group and a Spanish-speaking

Hispanic group. A local preacher or deacon from each group's culture presents a Bible study. The senior adults also have opportunities to attend two camps a year, one in the spring and one in the fall. For many of the attendees this is the only time they leave their neighborhood.

Barbara McCain sums up the attitude of volunteers and missionaries. "It is a wonderful feeling to know that you are not capable of doing this task, but then you sit back and see what God does through you. You do not have to know how you are going to do it, you just have to say yes to God and depend on Him for the rest."

Dora Hernández serves as the director of the Joy Baptist Mission Center. She began as a volunteer, working with food and clothing distribution. Tamara, the director at the time, noticed that Dora got along well with everyone, had a good attitude, and was a peacemaker. She asked Dora to be her assistant. When Tamara married and moved away, Dora became the center's director. She is a testimony to all the women in the neighborhood as "one of them" that God chose to lead the ministry.

Each Thursday, the Joy Center offers a worship service, followed by food and clothing distribution. Volunteer workers provide child care while parents attend worship and ESL classes. Twice a week the Joy Center is filled with children and teenagers roller skating and playing basketball. One morning a week adults can participate in an exercise and Bible study class.

Tae Kwon Do classes are another avenue of ministry at the Joy Center. One young man, Rubén Pinedas, accepted Christ at the classes. He had been hanging out with a gang and was about to join, when Christ radically changed his life. After more than a year of discipleship and spiritual growth, Rubén is now one of the assistant instructors in the Tae Kwon Do classes, and he teaches Bible studies at the center. A student at the University of Houston, Rubén is active in a local Southern Baptist church and is a shining example that the inner city has much more beauty and hope than many people think.

15

POWER TO RUN THE RACE

"Not that I have already obtained all this, or have already been made perfect, but I press on to take hold of that for which Christ Jesus took hold of me. Brothers, I do not consider myself yet to have taken hold of it. But one thing I do: Forgetting what is behind and straining toward what is ahead, I press on toward the goal to win the prize for which God has called me heavenward in Christ Jesus" (Phil. 3:12–14).

During the latter part of pregnancy and immediately following Abigail's birth, Dorcas and Emerson talked to the Baptist Mission Centers' Board of Directors about being coadministrators for the Baptist Mission Centers. Family life including a newborn baby, public speaking, and all the administrative duties the centers required had become more than one person could easily handle.

Emerson had strong paper and number skills, and Dorcas's people skills made her shine. They felt they could use their combined skills effectively and to the benefit of the centers. The couple proposed that Emerson handle the centers' administration, while Dorcas focused on speaking engagements and volunteer training. The board of directors and the Union Baptist Association approved. In January 1997, Dorcas and Emerson became coadministrators of the Baptist Mission Centers in Houston. And later that year, they discovered they would become parents again in early 1998.

Raquel Liand Byrd was born February 20, 1998. When Dorcas went into labor, she and Emerson were unable to contact her parents immediately. Dorcas was anxious, wanting her parents to know that their next grandchild was about to be born. Sensing that her daughter needed her, Carmen Camacho tried to call Dorcas and Emerson at home, but Dorcas was already at the hospital. Finally the two made connection. Both Dorcas and her mother marveled at the similarity between Dorcas's birth and her father's keen sense of God's presence, and Raquel Liand's birth and Carmen's prompting by God's spirit to call Dorcas.

Instead of taking work home, Dorcas and Emerson take their home to work.

Abigail, with her huge round eyes and sweet disposition, easily fits into work right along with Mom and Dad. She has a crib and swing in her parents' office. And Raquel Liand has filled both home and office with joy. Working as a family is ideal. Dorcas says, "I love having Emerson, Abigail, and Raquel Liand with me because it fits perfectly with my priorities in life. First comes my personal relationship with Christ, then my family, and then my ministry to others."

Emerson coordinates personnel and financial matters within the centers. But he most enjoys his ability to help churches connect with the community. Dorcas also works closely with the churches of Union Baptist Association, speaking and coordinating all volunteers. Together, the couple handle the external affairs of the three mission centers.

While Dorcas misses the constant one-on-one contact with people in need, she knows God is using her skills in the best possible ways. She dreams for volunteers to be able to present the gospel on a personal basis to each person who comes through the door. She looks forward to the day when volunteers can refer each person to other ministries at the centers, based on individual assessment and need.

Her father's words get her through each day. "Priorities. Priorities. Get your priorities straight, Dorcas."

Dorcas and Emerson have learned to work as a team. They accept each other for who they are, seeking to find faults within themselves before looking for faults in the other. During times of conflict, Dorcas and Emerson ask themselves, *Why am I not accepting his or her point of view?* They remind themselves and each other that God loves each individual and expects us to constantly grow more Christlike.

Carmen Camacho instilled a reality in her daughter that Dorcas wants to pass on to her daughters. These words, repeated to her so many times, still echo in Dorcas's ears. Now she can substitute her daughters' names in the affirmation.

Abigail and Raquel Liand, you are both unique. Nobody looks like you, acts like you, is you. God loves you. He has a special plan just for you. Polish the good qualities He has given you.